# *MANUAL 3:*

# COPING WITH LOSS

## EMOTIONAL AND PRACTICAL SUPPORT

## STEPHANIE OLDS

Printed in the United States of America
First Edition—Second Printing, May 2025

ISBN: 978-1968178109

Ink and Revival Publishing
Virginia, USA

# Welcome

Losing a loved one changes everything. The grief can feel overwhelming, and life may seem uncertain as you try to adjust to a new reality. When I lost my mother, I experienced just how difficult it is to navigate both the emotional pain and the practical responsibilities that come after a loss. There were so many things to handle—legal paperwork, financial matters, and everyday tasks—all while trying to process my own emotions.

Grief is different for everyone, and there is no right or wrong way to feel. But no one should have to go through it alone. This guide is here to help you with both the emotional and practical side of loss. It offers guidance on handling important tasks, finding support, and honoring your loved one in a way that feels right for you.

There's no timeline for healing, and no checklist that can take away the pain. But I hope this resource provides comfort, clarity, and a sense of direction as you move forward, one step at a time.

You are not alone.

## WHAT'S INSIDE

- ✓ **Grief and Healing** – Common emotions, the stages of grief, and coping strategies.

- ✓ **Supporting Children and Teens** – Explaining death in an age-appropriate way.

- ✓ **Handling Legal and Financial Matters** – Social Security, life insurance claims, and estate settlement.

- ✓ **Memorializing a Loved One** – Creating keepsakes, digital tributes, and ongoing remembrance.

- ✓ **Where to Get Help** – Support groups, counseling, and faith-based resources.

## FINDING YOUR WAY THROUGH GRIEF

Losing someone you love changes everything. In the days, weeks, and months that follow, you may feel overwhelmed—not just by emotions, but by the many practical tasks that come with loss. Grief doesn't come with a roadmap, and there's no one-size-fits-all way to navigate it. However, knowing what to expect and where to find support can make the journey a little easier.

Studies show that **nearly 57% of Americans experience complicated grief, where feelings of loss remain intense for much longer than expected** (American Psychological Association, 2023). For children and teens, the impact can be even greater, affecting their emotional well-being and even school performance. Yet, many families struggle to talk about grief, leaving individuals to process their pain alone.

This guide is here to help. Whether you're looking for ways to cope, needing support for children in your life, or handling the legal and financial responsibilities that come with loss, you'll find step-by-step guidance to make things just a little more manageable. Most importantly, you'll find reassurance that grief is not something you have to go through alone.

**Let's take this journey together—one step at a time.**

# Section 1

Grief and Healing

## Grief and Healing

Grief affects everyone differently. It's normal to feel sadness, anger, confusion, or even relief. Some common ways to cope include:

- ✓ Talking to close friends or family members.
- ✓ Keeping a journal to process emotions.
- ✓ Engaging in activities that bring comfort, such as listening to music or going for walks.

Grief is what we feel when we lose someone or something important to us. It can bring many emotions, like sadness, anger, confusion, or even relief. Everyone experiences grief differently, and that's okay.

Some people cry a lot, while others don't cry at all. Some want to talk about their feelings, while others need time alone. No matter how grief looks, it is a normal part of life.

Here are some practical ways to help cope with grief:

### 1. Talk to someone you trust
Grief can feel very heavy, but sharing feelings with a trusted person can help. Talking to a friend, family member, teacher, or counselor can provide comfort and remind you that you are not alone.

**Example:** If you feel sad about losing a loved one, you could talk to a grandparent or older sibling about your favorite memories with that person. Sharing stories can help keep their memory alive and bring comfort.

### 2. Write in a journal
Sometimes, it's hard to say out loud what we're feeling. Writing in a journal can be a safe place to express emotions. It can help make sense of thoughts and provide a way to let emotions out.

**Example:** If you're feeling overwhelmed, you could write a letter to the person you lost, telling them about your day and how much you miss them. This can help you feel connected to them in a special way.

### 3. Do things that bring comfort
Doing activities that make you feel safe and calm can help ease sadness. This might include listening to music, drawing, playing outside, or reading a favorite book.

**Example:** If you are feeling down, you could go for a short walk in the park while listening to your favorite songs. The fresh air and movement can help clear your mind.

## 4. Take care of yourself

Grief can make people feel tired, stressed, or even sick. Taking care of your body can help your mind feel better, too. Eating healthy foods, getting enough sleep, and staying active are important ways to support yourself while grieving.

**Example:** If you find it hard to sleep at night because of sadness, you could try creating a bedtime routine—like reading a book, drinking warm tea, or listening to calm music—to help you relax.

## Grieving Takes Time

There is no "right" way to grieve, and there is no set amount of time it takes. Some days may feel harder than others, and that's normal. Over time, healing happens little by little. It's okay to remember and miss the person or thing that was lost while also finding ways to keep moving forward.

# Journaling Prompts

Here are some journaling prompts that can help someone process their grief and emotions:

## Remembering Your Loved One

- What is your favorite memory with the person you lost?

  _____
  _____
  _____

- What are three things you learned from them?

  _____
  _____
  _____

- How would you describe them to someone who never met them?

  _____
  _____
  _____

- If you could talk to them right now, what would you say?

  _____
  _____
  _____

## Processing Your Feelings

- How are you feeling today?

  _____
  _____
  _____

- What emotions have been the hardest for you lately?

  _____
  _____
  _____

- What is something you wish people understood about your grief?

  _____
  _____
  _____

- What helps you feel comforted when you are sad?

  _____

  _____

  _____


**Moving Forward While Remembering**

- What are some ways you can honor your loved one's memory

  _____

  _____

  _____


- What is one thing you can do today to take care of yourself?

  _____

  _____

  _____


- How has this loss changed the way you see life?

  _____

  _____

  _____


- What are some things that still bring you joy, even on hard days?

  _____

  _____

  _____


Journaling doesn't have to follow a structure—writing freely about your thoughts and feelings can also help. The most important thing is to be honest with yourself and express whatever is on your mind.

# Section 2

## Supporting Children and Teens

## Supporting Children and Teens

Young children may not fully understand death, while teenagers may struggle with expressing emotions. Ways to help:

- ✓ **Use simple language** – "Grandpa died" instead of "went to sleep."
- ✓ **Encourage questions** – Let them talk about their feelings.
- ✓ **Include them in the process** – Allow them to attend the service if they want to.

When someone dies, children and teenagers may feel sad, confused, or even scared. They may not know how to talk about their feelings, and that's okay. It's important to support them in a way that makes them feel safe and understood.

### Use Simple Language

Young children may not fully understand what death means. Using clear and simple words can help them. Instead of saying, "Grandpa went to sleep," say, "Grandpa died. His body stopped working, and he won't be coming back." This helps avoid confusion and makes it easier for them to ask questions.

**Example:** If a child asks where their loved one is, you can say, "They have died, which means we won't see them anymore, but we can always remember them in our hearts."

### Encourage Questions

Children and teens may have many thoughts and feelings about death. They might wonder if they did something wrong or if they will lose someone else. Letting them ask questions helps them feel heard and supported.

**Example:** If a child asks, "Will I ever see them again?" you can say, "No, we won't see them in person, but we can remember them through pictures, stories, and the love they gave us."

### Include Them in the Process

Children and teens should have the choice to be part of things like funerals or memorial services. Being involved can help them say goodbye and understand what is happening. Let them decide if they want to attend.

**Example:** You can say, "We are having a service to remember Grandpa. You can come if you want to, or you can do something special at home, like drawing a picture or lighting a candle."

Grief is different for everyone, and there is no "right" way to feel. The most important thing is to offer love, patience, and a safe space for children and teens to share their emotions.

# Grief Support Worksheet for Children and Teens

**Name:** _____

**Date:** _____

**1. How do you feel today?**

☐ Sad

☐ Angry

☐ Confused

☐ Okay

☐ Other: _____

**2. What is one memory you have of the person who passed away?**

_____

_____

**3. What is something you would like to say to them if you could?**

_____

_____

**4. What are some things that make you feel better when you are sad?**

☐ Talking to someone

☐ Drawing or writing

☐ Listening to music

☐ Taking a walk

☐ Other: _____

**5. Who are three people you can talk to if you need help?**

1. _____
2. _____
3. _____

**6. What is one way you can honor or remember your loved one?**

_____

_____

# Grief Role-Play Script (For Parents, Teachers, or Counselors)

**Situation:** A child or teen is struggling to understand the death of a loved one.

**Child:** *"Where did Grandma go?"*
**Adult:** *"Grandma died, which means her body stopped working. She won't be coming back, but we can still remember her."*

**Child:** *"But why did she die?"*
**Adult:** *"When people get very old or very sick, their bodies sometimes can't work anymore. It's okay to feel sad or have questions."*

**Child:** *"I miss her."*
**Adult:** *"I miss her too. It's okay to feel sad. If you want, we can look at pictures of her or tell a story about our favorite memories with her."*

**Child:** *"Will I ever see her again?"*
**Adult:** *"Not in the way we used to, but we can keep her in our hearts and remember the love she gave us."*

This kind of role play can help children and teens feel safe expressing their feelings while also receiving clear, honest answers.

# Grief Role-Play Script (For Parents, Teachers, or Counselors)

**Situation:** A teenager is struggling with the loss of their sibling and is unsure how to talk about it. A trusted adult (parent, teacher, counselor) is there to listen and support them.

**Teen:** *"I just don't get it. One day they were here, and now they're just... gone."*
**Adult:** *"I know. It doesn't feel real, does it?"*

**Teen:** *"No. Everyone keeps saying it'll get easier, but it's not. I keep expecting them to walk through the door or text me."*
**Adult:** *"That makes sense. You spent so much time together—it's hard for your mind to accept that they're not coming back. Have you been able to talk about it with anyone?"*

**Teen:** *"Not really. Everyone acts like I should be okay by now. I don't even know what I'm supposed to say."*
**Adult:** *"There's no 'supposed to' when it comes to grief. You don't have to be okay yet. You don't even have to talk if you're not ready. But when you are, I'm here."*

**Teen:** *"I just feel so angry. At everything. At them for leaving. At myself for not saying goodbye."*
**Adult:** *"That's normal. It's okay to be angry. Losing someone you love is unfair, and it's hard to make sense of it."*

**Teen:** *"What if I forget them? I don't want to, but everything feels so far away already."*
**Adult:** *"You won't forget them. They were a huge part of your life, and that doesn't change just because they're gone. Maybe we can find ways to remember them—talk about your favorite memories, keep something that reminds you of them, or even do something in their honor."*

**Teen:** *"Maybe. I don't know. It just sucks."*
**Adult:** *"It really does. And you don't have to go through it alone. When you're ready, we can talk, or just sit together if talking feels like too much."*

This script gives space for the teen to express anger, confusion, and sadness while ensuring they feel heard and supported.

# Section 3

## Handling Legal and
## Financial Matters

## Handling Legal and Financial Matters

After a death, families must handle practical tasks, such as:

- ✓ **Getting death certificates** (needed for banks, insurance, Social Security).
- ✓ **Notifying financial institutions** (closing accounts, paying final bills).
- ✓ **Filing life insurance claims** (if applicable).

When someone dies, their family has to take care of important tasks. These tasks can feel overwhelming, but they help make sure everything is handled properly. Here are some important steps:

## 1. Getting Death Certificates

A **death certificate** is an official document that proves someone has died. Families need copies of this document to take care of things like bank accounts, life insurance, and Social Security. The funeral home usually helps get these certificates, but families can also request them from the local government office.

**Example:** If a family needs to close a bank account in the person's name, the bank will ask for a death certificate to make the change.

## 2. Notifying Financial Institutions

Families need to contact banks, credit card companies, and other places where the person had accounts. This helps close accounts, stop automatic payments, and pay any final bills. If the person received Social Security benefits, the Social Security office must also be notified.

**Example:** If a loved one had a credit card, the company needs to be told about the death so they can close the account and prevent extra charges.

## 3. Filing Life Insurance Claims

If the person had a **life insurance policy**, the family may be able to receive money to help with expenses. To get this money, they need to file a claim with the insurance company. They will need a death certificate and other paperwork.

**Example:** If a parent had life insurance, their family can contact the insurance company, send the needed documents, and receive money to help with funeral costs or other expenses.

These tasks can take time, and it's okay to ask for help from a trusted family member, lawyer, or financial advisor. Handling these matters may feel difficult, but they help bring closure and protect the family's future.

# Checklist for Handling Legal and Financial Matters After a Death

Here are a few items that can help guide families through these important tasks.

**1. Get Death Certificates**
- ☐ Request multiple copies from the funeral home or local government office.
- ☐ Use them for banks, Social Security, insurance, and other official needs.

_____
_____
_____
_____
_____

**2. Notify Important Organizations**
- ☐ **Social Security Administration** – Call **1-800-772-1213** to report the death if the person received benefits.
- ☐ **Employer** – If the person was working, contact their employer about benefits, payroll, and final paychecks.
- ☐ **Banks and Credit Unions** – Close accounts, stop automatic payments, and settle any debts.
- ☐ **Credit Card Companies** – Notify them to close accounts and prevent fraud.
- ☐ **Utility Companies** – Cancel or transfer electricity, water, gas, and phone services.
- ☐ **Insurance Companies** – Contact auto, home, and health insurance providers to update or cancel policies.

_____
_____
_____
_____
_____

**3. File Life Insurance Claims (If Applicable)**
- ☐ Find the life insurance policy documents.
- ☐ Contact the insurance company to start a claim.
- ☐ Submit the required paperwork (death certificate, claim forms, and proof of identity).
- ☐ Receive benefits and decide how to use them for funeral costs, bills, or savings.

_____
_____
_____
_____
_____

## 4. Manage Estate and Bills

☐ Locate the **will** (if the person had one) and contact a lawyer if needed.

☐ Pay any **final medical bills** or debts.

☐ Transfer property or accounts to the correct family members.

☐ Work with a financial advisor for any large assets or investments.

_____
_____
_____
_____
_____
_____

## 5. Handle Housing and Personal Belongings

☐ If they rented a home, notify the landlord and arrange for move-out.

☐ If they owned a home, contact the mortgage company or update ownership.

☐ Sort through personal belongings at a comfortable pace.

☐ Donate, sell, or keep meaningful items as the family decides.

_____
_____
_____
_____
_____
_____

## 6. Seek Support When Needed

☐ Ask a lawyer, financial advisor, or trusted family member for help.

☐ Take time to grieve and seek emotional support.

☐ Look into community resources for additional guidance.

_____
_____
_____
_____
_____

# Section 4

## Memorializing a Loved One

## Memorializing a Loved One

Many families find comfort in honoring their loved one's memory through:

- ✓ Creating a photo album or scrapbook.
- ✓ Planting a tree or garden in their honor.
- ✓ Holding an annual remembrance gathering.
- ✓ Making a donation to a charity they cared about.

When someone we love passes away, it can help to find special ways to remember them. Honoring their memory can bring comfort and keep their spirit alive in our hearts. Here are some ways families can do this:

### 1. Create a Photo Album or Scrapbook

Looking at pictures and memories can help us feel connected to our loved one. Families can put together a photo album or scrapbook filled with pictures, letters, and special moments they shared.

**Example:** A family might collect photos of their loved one and write down happy memories next to each picture. They can look at the album whenever they miss them.

### 2. Plant a Tree or Garden in Their Honor

Planting something that grows can be a beautiful way to remember a loved one. A tree, flowers, or a small garden can serve as a living tribute.

**Example:** If someone loved roses, their family could plant a rose bush in their yard as a way to remember them. Every time it blooms, it can bring happy memories.

### 3. Hold an Annual Remembrance Gathering

Some families choose to gather once a year to celebrate their loved one's life. They might share stories, light candles, or do an activity that the person enjoyed.

**Example:** If a loved one loved baking, the family might come together each year to bake their favorite dessert and share memories.

### 4. Make a Donation to a Charity

If the loved one cared about a special cause, donating to a charity in their name can be a meaningful way to honor them.

**Example:** If someone cared about animals, their family might donate to an animal shelter in their memory.

Memorializing a loved one can help keep their memory alive while also bringing comfort and healing to those who miss them. Everyone grieves in their own way, and choosing a special way to remember a loved one can be a personal and meaningful experience.

# Section 5

## Where to Get Help

## Where to Get Help

Support is available for those struggling with grief. Options include:

- Local grief support groups.
- Online grief forums and counseling services.
- Religious or community organizations offering guidance.

Grieving can be a difficult and lonely experience, but there are many places where people can find support. It's important to remember that asking for help is okay, and there are many options available. Here are some places that can help:

### 1. Local Grief Support Groups

Many communities offer grief support groups where people can meet others who are also going through loss. These groups are led by trained counselors or people who understand grief. It's a safe place to talk, share feelings, and listen to others.

**Example:** A local hospital or church might offer grief support groups. You can ask a counselor or trusted adult about groups in your area.

### 2. Online Grief Forums and Counseling Services

For those who may not be able to attend in-person support groups, there are online grief forums and counseling services. These can be found on websites where you can talk to others or even get professional help. Online support can feel easier for some people because it's more private and flexible.

**Example:** Websites like GriefShare or Crisis Text Line offer online resources where you can chat with others or a counselor.

### 3. Religious or Community Organizations

Many religious or community organizations offer support during tough times. Whether you belong to a church, mosque, synagogue, or other community group, they may provide guidance, prayer, and a sense of comfort.

**Example:** A church might have a grief support program or offer one-on-one support through a pastor. Community centers also often have programs that help people cope with loss.

### 4. Suicide Prevention Hotline

If you or someone you know is struggling with thoughts of suicide, please reach out for help. The **National Suicide Prevention Lifeline** is available 24/7 at **1-800-273-8255** (or

**988** for texting). You are not alone, and there are people ready to support you.

**Remember:**

Grief is different for everyone, and finding the right support can make a big difference. It's okay to talk to a parent, teacher, or counselor if you're unsure where to start. No one has to go through grief alone.

**Disclaimer:**

*I am not a psychology expert, and while I can offer general information about grief, it's important to reach out to a mental health professional or counselor for more specific guidance if you or someone you know is struggling with grief or mental health challenges.*

# After a Loss Checklist

☐  I have obtained copies of the death certificate (typically needed for financial and legal purposes).

☐ I have notified family and friends.

☐ I have contacted the funeral home to begin arrangements.

☐ I have reviewed financial matters (insurance claims, Social Security benefits, bank accounts).

☐ I have sought grief support (counseling, support groups, spiritual guidance).

☐ I have created a way to honor my loved one's memory (memorial, donation, annual tribute).


This checklist makes it easier for families to stay organized and ensure they don't overlook important steps.

www.ingramcontent.com/pod-product-compliance
Lightning Source LLC
LaVergne TN
LVHW082324080426

835508LV00042B/1536